Stephen Sandy was born and raised in Minneapolis. He has served in both the Army and the Navy. He holds an A.B. from Yale and a Ph.D. from Harvard, and is currently an Instructor in English at Harvard.

STRESSES IN THE

PEACEABLE

KINGDOM

STEPHEN SANDY

HOUGHTON MIFFLIN COMPANY

BOSTON   1967

FIRST PRINTING   W

Library of Congress Catalog Card Number: 67–15529

ACKNOWLEDGMENTS

Grateful acknowledgment is made to Mrs. Elizabeth Ames and the Corporation of Yaddo.

The author also wishes to thank the publishers of the following periodicals and books in which many of the poems in this collection have previously appeared:

Antioch Review, The Atlantic, Audience ("Near Marrakech"—copyright © 1958 by the Audience Press, Inc.), *Audit*

Best Poems of 1961 (Borestone Mountain Awards), *The Boston Review* ("The Waiting" and "Wintering in a Building Once an Ice-House"—copyright © 1966 by *The Boston Review*)

Carleton Miscellany, Caroms (Groton, 1960), *Chelsea, Chicago Review, Contact* ("Green Room," originally called "The Fledgling"—copyright 1960, Angel Island Publications, Inc.), *A Controversy of Poets* (Doubleday Anchor, 1965)

The Harvard Advocate ("Norway Spruce" and "The Boston Strangler"—copyright © 1965 by the editors and trustees of *The Harvard Advocate*)

Identity Magazine ("Circular in the Post Office," "Two Dimensional," and "Getting

For Al,
for Susan

CONTENTS

One

3 A Dissolve

7 Hiawatha

10 The Circular in the Post Office

13 After the Grand Union

16 The Destruction of Bulfinch's House

18 Thanksgiving in the Country

20 Can

21 The Woolworth Philodendron

23 Two Dimensional

25 The Ballad of Mary Baldwin

28 Her River

Two

33 Getting On

35 A Dream of Harm

37 Soaking

39 Celtic Law

40   In the Country of the Sudden Dance

42   From the Boston Strangler

44   The Sultan Wears a Crimson Turban

46   To a Father Feeling His Capital Gains

47   Near Marrakech

49   March Drive

50   Midsummer Nights

Three

53   The Norway Spruce

55   Boy, Blue

56   Breaks

58   The Waiting

59   The Grasshopper

61   Green Room

62   The Dancer

64   Watersheds

66   New England Graveyard

68   Hunter's Moon

70   Wild Ducks

71   Light in Spring Poplars

72   Stresses in the Peaceable Kingdom

Four

77   Doubling Back

79   "Power Flows to Trouble"

81   Et Quid Amabo Nisi Quod Aenigma Est

84   The Blind Accordionist

86   The Wallet

88   Driving Down to D.C.

90   Chantey for Minnesota under the Occupation

92   Home from the Range

96   Calculation

97   Catullus and Clodia

99   Reutlinger's Place

102   "A Tree in My Memory"

104   Wintering in a Building Once an Ice-House

ès

ONE

A DISSOLVE

The dream is tamed.
Fabulous bison of hunters'
memory, pumiced bone.

The idea
takes shape, virgin White Pine logged, stripped
clear to Minnesota.

It all dissolves,
the dying straggle in green fjords
of tall grass. They veer off,

the horses dying.

HIAWATHA

"These sacred objects had been in the tribe for many generations and were kept in the Sacred Tent of War. The changes following civilization led to the giving up of these objects, upon which the former ceremonies of the tribe depended. They were entrusted to the Museum by the chief of the gens, through Francis La Flesche and Alice C. Fletcher, 1884."

(Placard in a Harvard Museum)

1

False dawns
defunct as Jefferson and Monticello.
Skins of falcon wrapped in bladder, stiff
(brown paper, twisted), tied with sinew. A mauve
snuff box: "European manufacture."

They lie
locked in a case misty with handprints. Pale
lares and *penates* of tribes gone
to our reward. The painted bits call up
my bringing up in Minneapolis
(*city of water,* Ojibway & Greek),
haunt of Hiawatha
and his Minnehaha, whose stream once fell
dark past our home to its thundering fall.

There were no words between us then
when I followed my brother. Behind our fall
in the hollow we hid laughing,
quaffing the yellow mist; once,
dizzily bracing, gave streams of urine to the torrent.

Our selves. In that shade, shreds of sunlight and water
spattered us, held us. In that place we
were of it: outside was make-believe. Then
sun alone webbed our eyes; the misty
light walked on our legs.

We passed that sun-fired wall, boulder-
heavy, heavy enough to drag a boy down
in its scathing heave. Yet the sinewy whirl
skirling headlong from ledge lip high
up there fell inside to a soft
mist of embrace. Thought drowned in that grasp; **we**
                                        were
there, was all, contained by that cave, laid out
on the tawny stone. The white mane spumed light
into our stringy bodies: we shivered
sharing light's movement in our flesh.

And the Indian.
The Indian gave in
gave up his most sacred possessions.
Successful men, their hands in the till of the land,
gave up that fall. They
raised a dam's apron nine miles upstream:
a lake for a land development. Real
estate came first:
                    water grew less.
                                        Finally
only a stream, like bathwater from a tap,
roped down from the fall's brink.

                                        Then nothing.
Moss fumbled
over the rocks by the pool below; fish
rummaged in algae; the hollow
behind the fall, a dent bashed in the cliff
whose sandstone, worn by the force of waters,
sagged in creased swags like the belly
of a woman of many children.
The glen that had pooled fallen waters
was a rose of dust.
                         Then
an icicle.
                  We woke
cold to a perilous morning, one
beginning of us gone, a dream
which we'd been wakened from.

Upstream, two-by-four
wickerworks stapled the meadows;
barrows of formstone under the drifts
waited building weather. Blades
scored the tranced waters.

                         2

    Under the silver maples the young leaves
    have strewn grapes of sunlight. Ten yards
    upstream from the brink, leached gray and smooth now,
    the Indian's monument stands. I see him,

proud prince of the Onondaga
(Hiawatha, *maker of rivers*)
toting his princess forever; still he goes
over the dead creek bed: crisp leaves, pale stones.
His bronze arms hold her high so her toes
won't dip in the stream he fords alone
in the stream which is no longer there:
he walks where a mayor decreed he should,
a debris of benches, a brawl of picnics now.

Where the wind works patchwork napkins, and Saran
wraps wad at roots of elm trees, this Indian
commends to our Polaroid snaps, our immortal poses,
what was of what never was; himself.

Somehow: these relics got arranged here
— the sacred shell, worn by long use
in sacred ceremony; diminished skins
of martins, the meaningless holy pebbles,

the whole bag of pitiable tricks,
lean fetishes, these tinder bits, these
are some inheritance — not less
for lack of guarantees. We held

we held
that Hiawatha retained a nobility
which our minds had fashioned for our lives.

He was the instance on earth of essences
we held to have been the possible

condition of our lives.

    Hiawatha, tubercular, alcoholic,

    knew every lake and lair of game,
    guided my father on fishing trips,
    drank whiskey round the fire with the men,
    who chipped in twenty for the tip.

    One night, the winter of '56, he set
    home from the tavern, home from the hill.
    One last pull in the snow: then sleep.
    They found him brittle, immobile

    as bronze Hiawatha bearing his Penelope
    over the leaves in the park where children
    peer in casual disbelief at the god
    we made of what

    we most deeply believed, the sign of a profitable
    treaty with wildness; of something
    within, beyond us, too essential
    ever to be entertained in life.
                    The man

and his woman still cross the essential
stream of our youth, the stream which is
not there: for us, for him.
                    A death,
a truth, a childhood of us gone.

Teacher has told them another tale
the eyes of the children say:
they came for the fall, and it's not there.
But the boys accept, demand response; two
let stones fly, aimed at goldfish. Far-off
the plash is scarred by the suburb bus horn's squall.

And schoolchildren ramp each spring now
at the lip of the glen by that fall,
holding breath as their glances flow
over the rock ledge like dazzled water.
Here for the fall, they bridle, daunted, as gazes
slow into nothing, nothing but air.

THE CIRCULAR IN THE POST OFFICE

1

In a field in Maryland
in a vacuum cleaner box taped shut
        this boy was found.

The authorities not sure
of even his age — no trace of who
        his parents were,

no clothes, no name — just marks
of strangulation. They found his stare,
        his teeth, his sex

and now in post offices
on bulletin boards and city desks,
        all public places,

his naked faces stare
above the weight, the exact time
        when found, and where.

2

I turn away, but turn
again to watch this boy among
              the "Wanted" men.

I try to imagine the life
that ended up by hanging here.
              His photograph

has caught him once for all
on the wall crowded with crooks seen
              "Front" and "Profile."

Like a brown bag you pop
his paper skin is flattened there
              and shrivels up.

The black around his eyes
seems char, as if his life flared out
              in two quick cries

exhaling like a balloon
its substance, like a member spent
              and wilted down.

3

He had no father, mother
to call to in that night, and now
        there is no answer

to the authorities' demand
for parents. He sleeps among dark trees
        in unploughed land

and finds no father, mother.
The clue is a blanket round his knees;
        there is no other

in a field in Maryland
in the vacuum cleaner box taped shut
        where he was found.

The state's police declare
his height, his weight, the color of
        blue eyes, blond hair.

But all the authorities
who can't detect his killer, or what
        his name might be,

admit they cannot say
who thrust him into the world, or who
        forced him away.

AFTER THE GRAND UNION

You do not find much on a walk
in Saratoga now. The old
main drag lies low, like a tidal
flat or dry bed of a stream won
to deeper channels. The elms froze,
stripped bare by Dutch disease. Faces
on election posters moon down,
fat and forgotten.
               And the white
forest of columns, the long grove
of the hotel porches has gone
in steady, glacial withdrawals,
with pierglass mirrors and beveled
crystal chandeliers, like Christmas
trees, coiffing ormolu salons
of wrought rosewood and gold epergnes.

Empty for years, the Grand Union
where Victor Herbert played. Eaves where
twenty valets of Diamond Jim
were bedded down.
               The air where he

bet thousands on the final length
of a cigar ash
            hangs still and
smokeless, now Broadway is logged clear.
Pickers came and went. (Slater Brown
even secured the gilded trim
of Lillian Russell's bathroom.)

Yet time remains for horses, when
August and the rich arrive. They
treat their favorites to cool nights,
Canadian hay, the waters. . . .

One sleek girl, a won wife, from black
goggles high in her box stared down
the track, unflinching, observing
his family's entries; exertions
an aspect of her condition.
Star-nailed fingers touched a face stilled
like the face of Nefretete.

When the mansions turned cold the tall
light-limbed Negroes of the village
lidded the long Victorian
windows with patches of plywood.
Cross lawns of Skiddy von Stade's
immaculate, bandaged cottage
the wind released the gathered leaves.

One night, two thoroughbreds, pardoned
from their stalls, timidly ventured
in Union Avenue's headlights.
I watched them where they swam, dazzled
down that crystal rapids, away
to the dangerous dark; whinnying
for surer feet, for cooler nerves,
— sunlight perhaps, and simple fields;
brittle and frail, yet
                          surviving
in the cold of a mortal season.

THE DESTRUCTION OF
BULFINCH'S HOUSE

8 Bulfinch Place, designed and lived in by Charles Bulfinch, architect of the National Capitol; for years a tenement, it is razed to make way for government buildings.

His graceful swag blocks catch the eye,
but senses stall at whiffs of death . . .
antique cosmetics . . . urine . . . sweat
ooze from ruined windows and try
to grasp some walker through this breath
of air they won't give in to yet.

Outside, next door where Bulfinch built,
a silver nameplate on the door
I find caked black with sooty scum.
I pry at it. I rattle the bolt . . .
A woman calls from an upper floor
at her dog to stop. She strikes me dumb.

Inside Bulfinch's hollowed home
the nose goes gaga at more smells . . .
damp char and rust . . . here, haggard sheets
still on the beds — just risen from.
These personal effects excel
the remains outside in mangled streets:

mauled rooms bleed trash, not yet resigned
to emptiness. As if for a bomb

they fled — too rushed to pack — yet more
than glad to leave their lives behind,
as if not miffed to head for some
final occasion in the shirts they wore.

Nothing's removed but every sink!
A dumbbell rests by uncanned food;
and paper breasts, akimbo, boss
the room, beaming with lipsticked pink.
Only those scrawls of solitude
survive this small, survivable loss:

and yet I poke this man-made mess.
I guess what souls this mess has made
— and grub for a Bulfinch souvenir.
Here's one!
         Here's worth beneath the dross!
A handworked ceiling — plaster frayed
and cracked — but a lace of wreaths still clear.

Watch it! My grime goes white as the sieve
of a ceiling rains. Some witch up there
swears out. A hoarse bass spurts, *you go
to hell.*
      I see it's time I leave,
copping a doorknob and wondering where
in hell you tell people to go.

THANKSGIVING IN THE COUNTRY

1963

The twilight ascends into itself.
Clouds swim into themselves:
one cloud.

Night rises out of the long meadowgrass
reaches up
from among branches

these cedars take hands, a dark going.
One mile off, under the shade
of a larger limb

the headlights cross hands, blend
in a stream and
these drivers move

homeward round the interchange
round
and slowly somewhere.

He is gone. All these
boarded houses and bashed barns. Vanes
fallen in pumpkin vine

dry now. And morning
glories. This desire for someone
for our desires.

CAN

I found a sharp and jobless can,
now only fit to cut and scold.
It rang its tongueless gong of tin:
    rattling, rattled, cold.

Each time I kicked the thing its shout
echoed a bright, unopened youth.
Looking for work, it tossed about,
    one spiteful, jagged mouth.

Only a bent tin soldier, lame,
it went off crying to hold new food
(louder but lighter than it came),

    no heft, no shine, no good.

THE WOOLWORTH PHILODENDRON

Among the plastic flowers one honest one
graced Woolworth's floor: a real dodo in a green-
house of smilax and excelsior, a sort of proto-
gewgaw, if you please, it was so dada
in that museum of small cheers,
leaves snapped and torn by the sheer
relentless legs of ladies foraging
for comfort; in a plastic pot, the real thing.

Suspecting it alive, I brought it home.
Five months it sulked in a leafless dream;
through grillings by the daily sun it never broke
its dimestore trance, tight-lipped as rock.
And now it is April in the pliant bones and strange
to note the beaten juices fuse and plunge:
a green prong spirals up to the blaze, unplugs
revenge for ladies' grazing and ungrateful legs.

The shoppers' world is washed away — how fine
to see my green tooth cut the sunshine
and make a brittle pact with the sun's plan!
But it's more than the tender gesture of a jungle vine.

I watch it coil to careful multiplicity
through my weeks of boring work; I have begun to see
a careless wildness, long-leaved and green,
mesh with dark plots implicit in the sun.

TWO DIMENSIONAL

for Susan

Edging around her window shade
the sun flopped in and splashed orange,
a shape with movement, but no sound.
And yet each morning had its throat;
the cough belonged to the man upstairs.
He sputtered; tottered to put on pants;
she heard the door on the second floor
decide he was going — and the stairs agree.
Across their street he'd be opening
Angelo's Delicatessen Store.

His crowing dressed her with each sun
as the weeks worked by and winter came.
She heard him lock his store and climb
to the room above her room as the sun
fell sooner, sooner. The radiator
drummed like a solo drummer; thumped
deep in its workings, knocking the steel
like a knock on her door, like a latch
on a great door latching, latching.
The cough had softened . . . it had moved

— at least it sounded as if it had.
It seemed he had the third floor now.

And still at sun-up down he came,
across he went, tracking the snow.
And then one thaw in the dead of dawn
she woke to pull a blanket up.
Snow, and their street was white; outside
she saw the cough had gone away;
her delicatessen man and his store
had padlocks on the door. She wondered,
working her way through slush across,
where she'd go — now he'd up and gone —
for coffee and for bread. Inside
bright cans of food grew a fell of dust,
the door of his 'fridge hung loose, ajar;
all that ice dissolved at last.

She never passed the time of day
two minutes with him. Now all night
she plunders him and gets by heart
the sounds he made. As March moves in
crossing the land and climbing the sky
the sun comes. Slumber falls away
like a parade that passes by
without a band, the stillness leaving
a sense that fades of something long
gone by without its happening.

THE BALLAD OF MARY BALDWIN

On Third Street there's a naked spot
where a dead dog rotted the green grass plot.
What wouldn't they do if they found out who
    the person was who did it?
Ginny asked if there was a way
and Johnny too, to make it O.K.
Mother's not sure — not sure she's cross;
I still come running, and she's still boss
except what I do when she wants to know who
    the person was who did it.

    The grass is green, the roses are red.
    Do up the dishes and go to bed.

My father looked like he didn't hear,
but after he heard he shed a tear;
he swore what he'd do if I'd tell him who
    the man it was who did it.
I sat at my window and watched the trees.
I cried and said, "Do what you please."
Father and mother took the car,

they went to the city and went to a bar.
What else could they do? They didn't know who
    the man it was who did it.

    O the grass is green, and roses are red.
    Do up the dishes and go to bed.

I heard of a nurse in another town
who made no fuss and made no frown
and did it for you, if you forgot who
    the person was who fixed it.
I sat in the house for a week or so,
I didn't have the mind to go
until I thought it couldn't wait.
But she said, for her it was too late.
What should I do, and I so new
    and never before had done it?

    The grass is green, the roses are red.
    Dishes are dishes, and go to bed.

She said, some women four times a year
scrape out the motherhood they fear,
that's what they do, and they don't care who
    the people are who did it.
I found a doctor who said he could,
he shouldn't, but — for a price he would.
Next week the doctor went to his farm,

he slipped on a rock and broke his arm.
There was nothing to do when the one man who
   could do it couldn't do it.

   The grass grows tall, the roses red.
   Do up the dishes and go to bed.

Mother and father, Ginny and John
stopped talking, but their eyes kept on
saying what can you do when she won't tell who
   the boy it was who did it.
Walk to the corner. Walk by the lake.
People, people make me shake.
On Third Street I saw a naked spot
where a dead dog rots the green grass plot.
What good would it do if I did tell who
   the young man was who did it?

   The grass grows green, and roses red.
   Go do the dishes. Go to bed.

HER RIVER

It took all week, I don't know what it means.
Sun red and sexual and gone and I'm alone.
They will not tell me and their words are wrong.
Their helps are evening journals on the stream;
the branches broken like leaves along the storm.
This fish is tied in the bottom of the river.
And people are so careless with each other.
The rope in my throat, I don't know what it means.

It flowed all month, I don't know where it goes.
I broke my glasses, my feet go under snow.
The shell of that nut is horny but it's warm inside.
The lily pads bred corn-smut when they died.
O the moon weeps because it is white and gentle
and the wet cat claws me in the cradle of my arms.
The things they do, so careless with each other.
It takes so long I don't know what it means.

I let it ring and ring and do not answer, let
it ring and slice my ear drums, patiently.
The earth winces when they pull the cut elm down.
I burned my clothes. Grass grows in the sawdust place.

And up the pine the crane clings in the rain,
huddled against the trunk; sap clings to feathers.
Somewhere is no crowding; and there were children.
Things careless with each other take so long.

TWO

TWO

GETTING ON

One afternoon, finding nothing to do,
I barked at a dog from my window,
and the woman of the dog
told me for making a noise like that
I should be put in an institution.

I told her we worked on it, smiling,
and the woman told the police
and the man in charge of my building
informed me for the policeman:
no barking at dogs any more.

And every night in the park of sleep now
when the policeman isn't looking
and the woman of the dog is the other way
I bark at the beasts and they smile like spaniels
painfully trying to remember I'm there.

They are watching the flowers behind me; they hold
their soft mouths wide with silence.

The woman of the dog is looking: from her sleeves
her fingers grow, all leashes: looking.

I'll make a smile of teeth. I'll make my mark.

A DREAM OF HARM

In a dark house I was the guest;
in a damp bed I took my rest.
When dawn had steamed the wall I woke;
the breathless air: the window stuck.
Through a hazy pane I gazed on these:
orange cedar-apples on the cedar trees.

Some time I lay: in the room next mine
I heard her wash, get dressed, go down.
Above a bowl of milky stone
I rinsed my arms; they shed, they stained
the clear streams dark with grains of mould.
Around the bowl the black specks rolled.

Too thin to feel, grown through my sleep,
they bobbed beneath the spigot's pap
and clung to the stone above the drain.
I called, Come quick! I called and ran
down to her chair at the loggia door
and told her what, and told my fear.

We had to try to comprehend.
We stood before her washing stand.
With ladybug backs of orange and gray
they crawled in the bowl every which way.
What? we asked. What? Then, then we knew
— at the size of mice. And they grew and grew.

SOAKING

One microbubble of air
edges up my spine and
escapes at neckline;
the very lightest touch,
tick of caress,

tentative hand.
Farther down, the water
hot over my chin now
at earlobes, laps
in and out,

a warm finger in each ear.
The wet sole of my foot
rubs on the enameled rim
and sounds like a dog
whining to get in from the cold.

Down still more
the water round my face like a bonnet
various digestive workings

gurgle and clink
like steam heating.

I hear breathing,
a wind tunnel, loud,
breathe through the nose
deeply, a jet engine
taking its time

and below that
with even step
the heart
walks on the floor of the tub
firm and alone.

CELTIC LAW

The Lady's dispensation:
  to give the gold ring
  and a good harp
  to the lesser singer.

And his allegiance to her:
  to sing
  with meet quiet
  up to three songs:

Not disturbing his Lord's company,
  the Lord,
  or the Lord's
  Singer while he sang.

IN THE COUNTRY
OF THE SUDDEN DANCE

In the country of the sudden dance
I twined my arms above my head
and grew with leaves about my arms.
I let the touch of eyeless rains
run over me.
     I should have fled
from that sleep of trees. I dreamt of harm.

∾

The philodendron by my bed
has many arms and patiently
holds them aloft for easy alms.
Slowly alive, that aching head
ogles at heaven and sneers at me
shielding my eyes from day with arms.

∾

I'm roped in sheets and rigged with lights
— this morning torso tossed in dance
on the wreck of eight o'clock.

For still
in sleep I pound hot pavement. . . . Nights,
I find I lose three pounds. . . .
Those pants
wait like a job I cannot fill.

FROM THE BOSTON STRANGLER

Surely goddess born!

      Before taking her

blood

      in my arms   I

absolve her from drying

the dishes

          cup
her breast in my hand
          and
    so on
down

in

      Point of Fact

hung by my thumbs:
twisting her

arm behind

back I enter

Incognito,

the bad Barber

THE SULTAN WEARS
A CRIMSON TURBAN

May the Sultan behead whom he wants?

It is true the Sultan beheads whom he wants
when I go to the country of the Sultan
in a boat whose blades make the water play
like endless fingers on the belly rolling.

The Sultan squatting cross-legged in slippers
that taper to points that point at his head
puts down his mirror and nods, "Now
                    we will have beheading."

The Sultan beheading the people he wants
is holding his golden parasol cocked
and sipping his amber norman of lemon
and grenadine in beer.

The Sultan is taking the heads off
of people he wants — and more,
he hoists them on gates of palazzos, like brooches
on walls where the guards in red shoes guard.
These are the sights we have come to see,

I, and the tourists with eyes that take postcards
of all they barely manage to see.

We have come from a very afar
because a photograph in our head from a book
reminded us just in time of a desolation,
much time, long roads, great silence;
and sitting at the end of all our vacations
when the stakes of our makeshift trips are all pulled up,
there is the Sultan, under the trees
by a trestle table of the picnic area,
the Sultan who beheads the people he wants,
who is letting his swordblade shave his thumbnail

that ready blade, slipshod but shaved
shined, shampooed, and heady for bigger game.

TO A FATHER
FEELING HIS CAPITAL GAINS

Best to investigate the Taj Mahal
where twenty years the Shah Jehan
    built up a tomb to house
        his wife, Mumtaz.

Last lace of jeweled marble placed, the son
now runs the country. Jehan, put up
    in a tower over the river
        daily observes,

over the fields, the white domes bloom in the sun.

Locked in that rural marble while his boy
is playing the field, Jehan moans
    atonement for his untimely
        defiance of time,

the family grave. An exquisite pain. Below,
in shade, the sun blooding the hill,
    the footfall of the white ponies
        prancing toward Agra

lilts like a swallow into the brown sky.

NEAR MARRAKECH

Scavengers converge; the stricken
cow bequeaths its death to carrion;
the innocents at supper become their prey.

    Even the bones don't stay

put! Defeat pushes through the blue
heat-stained air, and beast heaves through
to rest; Time hovers, like a filthy wing

circling slowly down on the useful thing.

When faithful breath comes heretical
the penalty decreed is functional;
jackal and stray dog concur
to quarry every ounce of profit from the fur.

But fury that possessed one flesh still lives;
one crown of thorn in a dozen gullets thrives,

burns in the flapping birds; tears

through the well-fed cur that stares,
unable to bring himself to move, betrayed,

at the white handiwork his chops have made.

On the trampled grass a tide of white moves out;
sun dries all; contagious victory circles about.

Heat, swift and ubiquitous. Everywhere
flies settle through the golden air.

MARCH DRIVE

I was doing just fine just fine the tank was full
the punishment it took
                incredible
but having these late models with Special Drive
does not help keep an engine missing alive —
when something goes
                when something goes
                        no chains

suddenly you're up to here again
in mud . . .
              my bumper will not fit the jack
and with this Liquid Drive you can't quite rock
out of a spot.
              My paint job is a mess
what's more I like my body less and less
with this planned obsolescence for us all

— but then, my vehicle was designed to fall.

MIDSUMMER NIGHTS

The padded fingers held my ear,
her eyes grip as those paws, and stir
my blood. The cat's stare holds and says,
with glittering claws, *now put me down.*

ॐ

As carp and Northern Pike we caught
and father brained with pliers: white
discs of their eyes float still, float down
funnels of darkness, glittering green.

ॐ

From an unpaved road a deer leaps up
foaming in terror to escape
mounting my hood, the windshield, me;
splashing the pane through which I see.

THREE

THE NORWAY SPRUCE

Lifting itself from that hillside years
before his father lived, the spruce
rode in the rainy light.
The back years of its boughs
rolled from its feet, and his; arched in sprays up
like sowers' arms flung out.
Long generations worked a green
tangle on the slope below.

Save a lone sailor crow on a branch
scanning the approaching rain
from the black boat of his body,
the gardener stood alone
stood with crossed arms watching
watching until the patch of blue, down by the lake there,
moved.
A woman,
a woman alone running into the trees.
The man had thought he was alone there.
He'd thought so:
and turned to hoe the corn rows.

Laid in its dark bed the spruce
stood intently in the spaces it made of itself;
the man was trying to remember it:
she was alone. And the crow there
was sailing itself in the spaces
among the trees, calling *crow, crow*.

BOY, BLUE

By milkweed pod
and weeds' lobed leaves, nose down,
you nudge the sod, a mole-hilled world for bed.

On haunches rise,
and the sudden, dust-crocked light
starts in your eyes. One shadow over, hear

the cricket bend
to dogged zithering; from
a blue jumble of houses, hear mom's call.

Dad's car careens
with hollow clanks toward the house,
and angry screens harp back, and cranky hinge.

Riding the half light
the hawk streams carefully home,
a dusty mouse in his shopping bag of hands.

Boy, blue, go back,
your yellow spoonbread waits.
Their workday must be hashed; your meal grows black.

BREAKS

You and I together — like that!
On broad sunlit uplands hand in hand.
Whole weekends at Shangri-la;
they give us a white room
the Himalaya in snow out the small, high Mediterranean window

our hearts' walls are white
in the winds of darkness and silence

love smokes from the hills of sleep
and yet when I go down I cannot even remember
the long outlines of your face
the marvelous celadon bowl of your voice.
It is the time, the space between us, wins.

Somehow the faith (what
word you feared most)
between us needed — I don't know. What
tensile strength? Now, now
I cannot remember your face!

How difficult to move, they say, a cobweb
not the web,
single simple strands, delicate one by one,
not these so much
but the hardest part is keeping the
spaces in between right.

It is the time, the space between us, wins.

THE WAITING

Mute noons, mute afternoons, the pride reclines
in shades the poinciana's limbs can manage,
flaking the light.
                    They stare. Each blink occults
the wide savannah blurring in their eyes.

Consider: the matted locks of the lion. It is
a bush where dark, forgotten triumphs nest.

In the zoo that morning the coiffed brute pondered
us. He touched his drooping whiskers with a paw
that hovered tenderly. The paw hovers
tenderly, as if the whiskers were wounded.

THE GRASSHOPPER

Huddled, crouched there on the cement
it looked as if the highway hurt
    him, the braided brown
    left leg one half inch
farther left than the right was right.
Each vault the grasshopper took ahead he took
two left — or right — or backward. All
his progress seemed to lack a goal.
        Did he fear cars —
humped there like a crunched horse-chestnut?

What had gotten him down? He snapped
and leapt, dodged gusts and spaces; cracked
    his legs on cement,
    rough as a strip of
Brobdingnagian sandpaper,
(scraping the spun, slowly diminishing cars
that whined to chrome bits down the ends
of the earth). He hopped three feet right
        into the lane.
Then stopped. Then back to the shoulder

twenty inches grass-ward on packed
gravel. He shone out in the crisped
    October light like
    buffed cordovan! Had
he been (I couldn't tell) the green
and summer kind, turned mulberry like maples,
turned by the long season closing?
He leaned, eyeing (perhaps) my leg;
    his great joints cocked
ready to pitch from any harm.

In the lane then, rooted. Waiting.
I, there, spitting at him, hoping
    he might think me rain
    and be on his way.
I scanned the distances home; rain
after all! It would! And what was this drained thing
to hold me, catch me in the wet?
Right there: I thought of the friends whose
    time could be mine.
Why stay out? Why do I do it?

GREEN ROOM

He bristles softly for the shape that comes.
Quilling for wind (his war, whatever calms)

the squalling in him tantrums toward a song,
and flight shall stick yet to that penguin wing.

Brief bangle wings, frail token of the bird,
muddle his studies to don birdhood;

though gusts break twigs, and more, he still shall **sift**
for himself, when fastness comes loose aloft.

A boughless highness court him! where
heaven shall obscure which twigs were

his mother's thighs. And he, welcome,
may stop again some day in this green room.

THE DANCER

On scent: of something
in the distance, unseen,
devourable, our glad stray

trots down the to-us-
invisible ribon
something's left behind to be

followed. The dog's nose
keeps its pure consciousness
of quarries in general

wholly unable
ever to stop sensing
them, even in sleep. Open,

opening to what
has gone on before, it
calls figures for the dancing,

the unwitting legs.
The mongrel is master
of method in his running,

for whatever it
purely may be out there
need never be downed for its

pursuit to keep him
conscious of a presence
pure, and wholly durable.

WATERSHEDS

The upper lake, by its
    convulsing trickle
fell, the packing culvert's torsions heaved white
water crumpling, and hourly became
the lower lake: the upper unaware
of its depleting of itself or what
deep transmigration inadvertently
        was making there,
        under the road between,
as a slow seeping; — to what succeeding
body of water it would give itself.
        That afternoon
        in the late year's sleek light
both lakes looked gravid, blank with a sluggish
dignity; neither by the least ripple
acknowledging it was becoming more
or less than itself. The upper might have
been a father, tightlipped, grim to see his
        son change body,
        his kindred wax and wear
his old sinews in the sun, as a young
spore flies the flag of its diminished seed.

Spray lathered and leapt up
atilt and strewed itself
down gullies of light; coiled to gloss the air.
The grave bodies, the tumble vying with
sunlight between, made a fit relation
in that serious process: no party
acting agent, each into predicate
of its nature
as the seasons followed.
But perhaps that upper lake (as father)
had no sense, had no need to acknowledge:
for it, from deep
springs or distant hills was
being refreshed with a clearer liquid.
And the lake below, the darker waters
screened by the hills from the declining light,
were fulfilling themselves, already were
spilling themselves below the surface
at some mouth not
recognized, not charted,
to the valley below, all the valleys
and plains beyond, and to a distant sea.

NEW ENGLAND GRAVEYARD

Back of the church the busy forsythias bow
and scrape to May and all these blessed stones
stiff in their careful finery of words;
the mess of markers makes me go and browse.

Somehow the blocks of slate and marble hate
to be cut and carved to the dimensions
of Mary Monday's age and her virtues.
At heart they hurt to be made literate
and they are rebelling, fast as they can,
shedding an edge, a letter, as they go
— a year, a part of a skull, a bone —
it hurts them to stand so long for this
kind of death not theirs. Fast as they can
they are leaning away from their duty
and look down longing for the warm sod.
The prides and fears they stand witness to,
the ladies and gents, are only whimsy now.
They cease to reflect that wary pride
the flesh beneath them took in lying down.
To the last date line and death's-head stare,
the legend reads, "There! I've done it!"

But these are only beginning,
the blocks of shale forget their lines
letting the sunlight and rain divide
and subdivide their veins and bone.
They do not care, they only feel
an unnatural heaviness, tottering so
in the hot light. They long to be off and away,
they toss and jibe in the sun;
a whole regatta of black sails, they are sailing away
over the lumpy green yard of time, and never
coming about for home until they capsize
turned turtle by boys from Central Square.

Tired of holding — they are tired of holding up;
their always-leaning makes me hold my tongue
and sit with them awhile. We heave
our shoulders, or our shadows, on the mounds,
while under the hills, memorials more fine
lie lip to paper lip
                     and keep their impossible word.

HUNTER'S MOON

An airborne dragon-
fly brash with first frost
buzzed me where I lay
in the open, still,
considering a
juniper lap and
vein the clouds;
                    floating
like seaweed or a
mote down the eye's film,
he stained the sky with
four mica-seamed wings,
just able to hold
onto his outrigged
eyes, spying — a head?
— a stone?
            Circling or
in the sunless air
coasting he hovered
the wing whirr missing
flaking, taking me
again — his insect

candor! — and again
for a window, a
door, a sun-banked stone,
or any warm thing.

WILD DUCKS

Nine mallards amiably swim
the stream's treadmill. Sedate,
intent; bills front, they form
a *V* unmoving as kites

swimming the unseen wind.
Upstream they go together;
they glide as if upstream
some hand guided them there.

With button eyes not looking
they move, unmoved, in the pull
of taut, positioning strings,
the hand's extended will.

LIGHT IN SPRING POPLARS

A populace — but
of one blood. Contagious,
one, the sun
in the white poplars flared, radial, foamed

infecting through, when
up cold marches of the
slow season
buds caught; waxed in the pealed light, as the sun

on far flaked waters
was one husked candle
furled to light
others; — the gold buds many, but one flame.

STRESSES
IN THE PEACEABLE KINGDOM

1

Dahlia's gold explosion,
Queen Anne's lace in seed: wide

lattice, brittle grid: where
sleep divides, divides
                  ripe
melon ripening still, a
fulness splitting
               elders
dancing, 'remembering
but not affecting youth'

vegetables smiled, and
Adam saw fervor, saw

his age a smoulder wrought
and rallied by the sun.

2

The Garden of Eden,
remember, was only

a garden to Adam
as he trod long shores
                    the
fallen breaker, the white
sand, the green wall of trees:

then Adam wandering
toward his evening, released

upon the host his earth,
and time: first companion

limits! For Adam, for
atom, bursting forth, an

energy unleashed upon,
informing the waste world.

FOUR

DOUBLING BACK

Thirty miles for a bag left behind
remembered
fifteen miles

on my way: I must go fifteen more
to the next
exit. I

pay, of course, fifty cents, U-turn, and
pick up my
ticket East

and retrace my first path, finding hills
and snow fields
another

way, the sun over my shoulder now,
not above
my eyes, pay

to get off, retrieve the left baggage:
I am free
to take on

another ticket, turn into the
old approach,
merge with cars

which were once sixty miles behind my
own, and head
West once more.

"POWER FLOWS TO TROUBLE"

November, 1965

Machinery dials
in the candle light
made fierce faces; said
nothing, nothing. The
voltameter's brass
lorgnette blinked: zero

— then less. From the street,
upstairs, we gathered.
Then lit more candles.
Their burrs hatched yellows,
and Mrs. Fassett
became Agatha,

Mr. Sweeney, Jack;
Miss Wilson, Rosalind.
Then laughter, with no
apparent cause. We
laughed until tears gave
the candles halos.

When the lights went out
we did not know how
big a failure we
were part of: but when
the News resumed its
usual composure

we put the candles
out
and ventured, one by
one,
into the dark and
evening engagements.

ET QUID AMABO
NISI QUOD AENIGMA EST

Then watching the unposed beggars pose
I saw the subjects that occasion offered him
doubtless never intrigued the master
as they intrigue us:
Harvest, the Kermesse, Justitia, Skating.
He took down suffering — and those insanely
rush-hour comments on where some action was —
first as a means to chaffer his betters, those
lumpish onlooker burghers, too often viewed
at a distance.
                Obviously, though, he was
moved by dolts; the highly sketchable maimed;
the cloaks in which you feel fleas mincing
and see where rats, by night, nibble. Just what
inner occasion let him see things —
                things as they were
is not clear; only that he needed them.

Take "Blind Peasant, Begging" — the dazzled eye,
wild stare of a winter deer begging food or
safe passage from where he's been cornered. But
smiling, incongruously — a wily smile,

up-to-no-good, you think. Yet the whole body
in rapt and freehold peace. Not ignorance, this
indifference to the pains which make him up.

Or take all these little fellows
clumping about with hats over their eyes
all looking squashed, like dwarfs, chin flush with chest
and neck sinking its root in shoulder thew:
this swirl of dying dancers might have been called
"Ataraxy Among the Accident-Prone"
or "Survival Through Indifference, as seen
in the Peasants of Breughel."
After so many
scrapes as patently planed their knotty faces
the living showed through; lives, like their profiles,
gathered a certain definition from
cold fires and dry trenchers. Chill days grew light
and marvelous when each get circumscribed,
like three-time losers the second time around.

I thought of others: people I knew, whose smiles
stolidly flickered like home movies; some who
displayed lapsed attitudes, say, toward going out
in the rain (without coat or rubbers) all day;
the crowded minds, decreeing against the crowd,
or sailing alone at night in rising weather.

Madness may well
be a crowded mind. But fury comes to the

stripped life. The soul that would survive its strife
grows
        accident-prone, carefully careless
with its flesh. — Not the stink, taste,
the sore of having been so wanting long,
the dizzy or the colic of haste

                it is the *against,*
the gainsaying of the hap bidding
hapless to death's gain: deathward, weighted,
wearied sunless, the cringing, the hulk strange
of a presence, a space change, a win time dons
when you gag in the gorge of the timing,
the falling, the false surrender:
sleeping in doorways, sailing alone at night,
who wryly bear their limps, their abdominal
pains, all mornings after, hanging and hanging,
lousy shirts, the pocked forearm, and scarred wrist.

THE BLIND ACCORDIONIST

Bass. Counter-bass. Seventh. Love
chinks in the measuring cup.
He sings straight
past you, calling. His career
is to be believed.

Like a slow child he learns
what patience is; learns
the turnings of his halls
— not knowing when halls turn.
Grows outward slowly
to what spaces chance his way.

A day reminds him of the movements in his mind
a night unminds him of. He goes
swaying his way among deep waters —.
He knows currents of pavement; curbing; rain
splicing gusts and his hair.

He gains himself
by canny polkas at sunny corners.
First in his walk-up to demand

good lighting on the stairs
— he knows absurd mazurkas.
The TV in his room is there
most honorably.

Stools at counters, stalls;
the escalator; doors revolving
are the waters the world puts round him;
the public garden Sundays, the bush
of marjoram. He inches
into presences. They receive him.
They take on his weight. He sings.
They are there.

There they are, embracing him
the way a man who steps into a river
finds out the river as it works around him
showing its force, its substance, flowing.
The world afoot embraces him,
river, deep water of his life:

no shape but what its banks, its hulks,
its pilings give.

THE WALLET

Moping down, I watch fence posts
knitting the cut fields
like stitches in old skin.
In love, I'd find this beautiful.

Slogging these bottom acres I think
back to each girl & season since fifteen.

Not the names:
the lot.

Scaling a barbed-wire fence my wallet
still fat with mumps of numbers and cash
pops from my hip.
I stop,
climb gingerly back.

It lies in a cradle of field grass and cosmos.
The sky waits, and the fields hold still.
Whorled mats of couch grass and cosmos stalks

wild oat and barley
glisten.

Held in black leather
plastic reflects the sky like a puddle.
The road is still. The wind dead.
A face grins up.

2

For a moment I think of leaving
the whole business behind:

the Washingtons with Mona Lisa frowns,
the seeing-eye pyramids that
do help me get there and back.

All this is mine —

dog-collar cards to show officers
who I belong to
and snaps, the smiled-in faces

— is me: and I pocket all

knowing I'd lack my past
like losing a cast on a broken limb
too early.

DRIVING DOWN TO D.C.

My father always drove fast
or slow as he wanted

if they pinched him
they pinched him, a
ticket was a ticket

                THIS IS AN
            EVACUATION
                ROUTE

if they fined him he paid.

And *Away He Went* as fast
or slow as he wanted, & now

                SPEEDERS
                LOSE
                LICENSES

on the John F. Kennedy Highway

                    the meadows
I remember
              the meadows grow faint
those old A-merican meadows
                    where the corn
where sweet
under the wind-burned sky

the suede wheatfields, the sweet
distances a boy brought up keeping
the back seat quiet remembers

                    THERE ARE NO
                    SERVICES   ON
                    THIS HIGHWAY

the Susquehanna . . . wide
of channels, various with
islands
              sea of light . . .

                    BELAIR

                    RISING SUN

                    ELKTON

                    WINTERS RUN. . . .

CHANTEY FOR MINNESOTA
UNDER THE OCCUPATION

We are landed. Safe. The bishop is dead
though. Or dying.
                             He cannot be saved.
I am holding his head, his head in my lap
but the bald skull is cracked
like an old china bowl.
                             There the laced surplice
is dabbled with blood, the Red
Cross fails here and we won't get out without
papers.

The lieutenant by the wire door again
is explaining again
about passports and loyalty and
the proper incisions and shots.

And I do want the letters from someone I love,
I peer in the long slash on his crown,
it is bald there, and maybe death for him
and yet my fingers prise, there seems a lot
of room in here, pull for a better purchase

— ah here! My letters and our passports
tight with a rubberband from *Triple-M*.

HOME FROM THE RANGE

I can hear the dour howl of far
breakers from sea shells held to my ear

and deep from my skull I hear the
same small, inveterate tolling
— I've come of age!
     America,
a screened knowledge;
       the bad duty
serving one's country.
      My head is,
the waste is, not clear; is a sound
rings like the sea in my ear,
        rings:

  "Minuscule nerve ends of the inner ear
  abraded by a rough sound," the doctor said,
  "you will be deaf in the highest ranges;
  no matter, you won't miss everyday sounds;
  hear talk, the usual noises, music . . ."

"Flag is up — Flag is waving — Flag

is down."
                    The bolt slides home in my
head a slender explosion —

but a fist's distance from the ear.

                        ৯৯

Waters rolling, the sound of war,
heavy traffic on wet pavements
the far-off highways
                        the plains, the
straddled sanctuaries
                        the fast
wildnesses hooped, roped like
                                horses
being broken, the lasso of
highway, concrete belt, the sing of
vans
        cars escaping into space

such as Merton and his brothers
hear from their dark dormitories
Kentucky nights . . .

                        ৯৯

The sound, the guns
(said the Fort Knox private who knew)
was the sound of sea
          heard inland —
heard as immortal agony
as galactic matter earthbound . . .
of God
      in his generations
wild. Crashing against the shore of

our flesh, womb-wrought curl of ear,
natal memorial, chalice
of delicate lobes:
          "Ready on
          the Right
              Ready on the Left
          Ready on the
              FI-RING LINE . . ."

     ह

Nothing
          nothing will clear this waste;
guns of unlearned knowledge toll.
                        Arms
hold me with a light G.I. ring;
a slight ear-plug, always in place.

At Gethsemani
                    Merton hears
the guns of Fort Knox. The ring of
sea
          the sound of the traffic down
the inmost canals of our life.

                    ૐ

Srrrrriiiinng —
                    "Always
be deaf in the highest ranges."

CALCULATION

She comes closer and says, "poor child
you haven't enough for a family,"

    her wish, a tendril, groping

"I dreamed the world once for you, poor boy,
now my dreams are as pale as the desert

    my heart is forgetting you

I have wasted with waiting, my son."
She closes her checkbook, sighing; and then

    flies down to Tucson, dying.

CATULLUS AND CLODIA

Thinking of him and his poems in these woods
I hear the elms creak when the lumbering wind nears,
October trees like old women in rocking chairs
aged and speechless, mouths ajar.
Clodia gave carelessly
as an elm paying out what no longer concerns it
while Catullus, saucy always, (but
ardent at last, ardent) ran
to vent sleek postures through those drifts.

ॐ

The trees are leaning from burdens the wind brings to bear,
I poke in the undergrowth; everything
smells like rain. Suddenly the trunks are loud above me;
they bend, black doors creaking. And yet,
of course, they never unhinge,
blacker and taller every year.
                    Poems
more than her wooden freedoms were his gain;
his love kept coming at her, passing through
in a return as helpless as these yearly storms.

૪ુ

Buds. Recurring splinters *from*
the straight grain. Each line,
stem from the frayed end of passion.

Her carelessness a shaft that ground
down splintering into flesh. Unspoken wounds.
But they worked back, for him, to his surface,

each wound the first, each difficult
in the way that every autumn is the first
and unremembered in the grain when sharp buds vault toward
   sun
probing their speechless twig.

REUTLINGER'S PLACE

δός μοι ποῦ στῶ

Under Reutlinger's oak I watched
the flash rain storm
pummel the maples on Mt. Hope
   — not much of a
mountain! small enough to be owned,
this South slope by
my friend; the North, by old Cyrus
Weatherby. Gusts
swirled the under-leaves, white, a brightness
   on the fresh wind!

ȝ⸱

Under dogwood and lilac gone
   halves with fern lay
poison ivy, the small arms oiled
   waiting and green.

ȝ⸱

The old farm house,
long mess of 2 x 4's and loads
   of thick sheetrock;

under hewn rafters, sleeping bags.
   Gone in the shakes
the barn no longer remembers
cattle — but mice;
bursting its boards now with sofas
   blankets and books.

ৡ

Two delighted dachshunds and the
   two-year-old child,
through the slow descending summer
   of yellow peals
on worn oak or maple door sills,
forget — and learn
old bonds of house-training once more.

ৡ

   Strong John Tobin
had broken his winch. He smiled while
his thick hands clenched
above four hundred cement blocks
   two at a time.
"My fault, I should have oiled the thing."

ৡ

   We helped out: then
on workclothes shadows of certain

    shapes long parted
showed through talking over home-brew —
    (balding khakis,
gray fatigues: of Fifth Cavalry,
Corporal chevrons,
the old Yankee Division shield) —
    talk of how much
for bricks, new or scrubbed, per thousand.

"A TREE IN MY MEMORY"

I found it one morning,
shelving numerous gold shoulders windward.

The furrowed trunk stood clothed
in ribboning bark that clung from its sides.
Rough shags curled lithe and wide
all the way down from the helm of the top
lapping and spraying down —
not wood, but water flowing down its trough
of leaves — as if a dark
fall, pitching for earth and root from zenith.

I wanted the name for
such a mastering of mortality,
of standing still without
appearing to. I took leaves and went to
the man who's known this land
forty years:

            that hickory! — he knew it;
and laughed, when he tossed me
a worn old book where it was written up:
". . . the nuts fall, and schoolboys

have marked the tree their own, and are on hand
to bag the crop to the
last sweet nut, if squirrels do not thwart them."

And I might gather some
I thought, an October woodsman thinking
of "Snow Bound" and cider.
Back I went: around it the dead twigs lay,
long grass, and shrunken there
some few quartered husks of the angled nuts.

I read this; I was warned;
someone, who took no chances with weathers
or other harvesters,
had stripped each nut, picked up the drops, and stored
his crop for winter. He
was in the habit: I was not — and found
my nature with a book.

WINTERING IN A BUILDING ONCE AN ICE-HOUSE

Neatly reprieved from ice, this
   house part ice-house still:
sawdust-packed studs keep snug the
   space they once held cold.
Outside, sparrow and junco
   worked a crude feed stand
convinced that I, inside, would
   not preach to them. They
lacked time.
            Still, they took their time!

   Junco and sparrow
of black, boreal forests
   peered equatorward,
possessionless, in at my
   unseasonably
temperate zone of comfort.
   They did not mind me
staring back, marveling at
   their quick regardless
isolation from their deaths,

their timeless song,
timeless hunger of their cries!

    I am rooted, I
perish in their eyes like summer
    under my warm clothes!
— hang on, hang like a spider
    guarding the space he's
wired off to supper from
    — or like the winch nailed
to this ice-house gable, which
    (strutted to swing-lift
clean-sawn blocks from the cleared lake
    inside)
           hangs there still.